Negotiation Pocket Tips

Learn to negotiate at a glance

Paúl Fraga

To my father

To Emilie

To my mother wherever she is

Table of Contents

I

III

INTRODUCING THE 'ELEPHANT IN THE ROOM'

Why a negotiation book? Because negotiation exemplifies very well the syndrome of the **'elephant in the room'**. That is, **when there is a situation where all participants are aware of an evident truth, but which, however, we deliberately ignore.** Negotiation is a discipline, an issue of our lives, that usually we pay no attention to in our day to day. It happens every day discreetly but also consistently. Negotiation is always there even if we don't realize or don't want to see it. It's stubborn. It never disappears.

We negotiate constantly. With our partner, with our children, at work, with friends ... It seems that we don't do so, but the truth is that we negotiate unconsciously. Without knowing it. That's why it is so important to know how to negotiate. Because it is especially relevant.

However, **there are very few things that we do so often and to which, consciously, we give less attention**. Being honest, I don't know the exact reason for this behavior, although I can guess what could be. Negotiating is a skill that generates suspicion beforehand. It generates certain mistrust in the negotiating activity itself, but also in the skill each person believes to have to carry it out. As far as I can remember there are few disciplines that are so affected by prejudices and self-imposed barriers.

Very often is the concept that we have of ourselves that drives us to put the 'handbrake'. And we do it with the false belief that this attitude has no consequences. And there is nothing further from reality. **Avoiding the secrets of negotiation, consciously or unconsciously, invites us to go throughout life without guidance**. From a comparative point of view, it is enough for someone with whom we interact to know, even very succinctly, some negotiation techniques so that we voluntarily, and willingly, do what that person wants us to do. Because, partly, negotiation is about that: making other people do, willingly, what we want them to do.

But isn't that manipulation? No, it is not. Manipulation is exclusively unidirectional and, therefore, brief. With little margin. Negotiation is, however, bidirectional. **Both parties doing things with a true interest in doing them. That's the goal**. Both parties doing things with conviction. Both looking for long-lasting relationships. A thing that, being honest, doesn't always happen.

On the other hand, regardless of whether there are personalities with a natural predisposition to negotiate, the truth is that negotiating is something that can be learned. This book is a good proof of it. There is only one issue that is not related to any learning process but which is nevertheless the trigger for everything else: the conscious acknowledgment that one is immersed in a negotiating process.

At this point I will try to convince you, dear reader, that negotiation has a lot to do with technique, but also with psychology and 'theater', in the good sense of the word. In short, negotiation is a game whose rules should be well learned.

Now, do you dare to be a good 'player'? I guess so. Let's begin!

PART I: THE OUTER GAME (TECHNIQUES)

1. "IF YOU REQUEST SOMETHING, WHAT ARE YOU WILLING TO GIVE?" (ROBERT KIYOSAKI)

NEGOTIATION IS AN EXCHANGE GAME. A scenario where it's not about succumbing to a gradual surrender process. Complying with the counterpart demands has nothing to do with negotiation. That is an exercise of submission. It is true that conceding is something fundamental, **however concessions must be given in exchange for something. Always**.

There are frequent the episodes where, throughout a negotiation, one part, usually very experienced, acquires a stubborn position standing one's ground. With this type of behavior, an inexperienced negotiator tend to concede successively what the counterpart asks for, in the hope that such exercise of generosity pities the opponent so he may end up conceding any of his requests.

However, reality is very different. Determined positions are typical of experienced negotiators who see on the other side a candid and inexperienced 'soul' that could leave aside the objectives pursued in the negotiation in order to try to get along with the opponent. They are typical tricks of that person who knows well what the game rules are and uses them selfishly.

4

Therefore, yes to concessions as long as something is obtained in return. If I give something the counterpart has to give me something. And in the opposite sense as well. If I ask for something I must be ready to grant something.

That being said, what can I grant in return for my requests? It is here that the principle of hierarchy acquires a special relevance. As a negotiator, you must fight to obtain what you desire most in return for the least harmful concession for your interests. **While the order of the objectives you pretend should go in order from highest to lowest, your list of possible concessions should have the reverse order, that is, from lowest to highest**.

We shouldn't forget that things have no value themselves. Things have the value they are given. It is relative. Thus, when faced with the same issue, the value granted by each party may differ importantly. Consequently, it would be about obtaining what has the greatest value for me within my pretensions, granting to the other part something that has little or no value for me. However, the value for the opponent of that same element I'm granting can be very important. So we can find ourselves facing a scenario where one part can make a request of great value for that person, but which has very little value for the counterpart, so he would have no problem to grant an element that is irrelevant to him but tremendously important for the other part.

"NEGOTIATION IS EXCHANGING. IF I GIVE SOMETHING THE COUNTERPARTY MUST GIVE ME SOMETHING, AND IF I ASK FOR SOMETHING, I MUST BE READY TO GIVE SOMETHING"

2. "EVERYTHING HAS ITS LIMITS" (QUINTO HORACIO FLACO)

When I talk about limits I mean that **when negotiating everyone has to have clear what is going to be the range where he will be moving in**. It is about establishing clearly in the previous periods what I am looking for in the negotiation, what I expect. In the same way you have to determine very clearly those issues that you don't want to give up. In other words, what elements are not likely to be traded.

These two things are key elements to consider: WHAT DO YOU EXPEXT AND WHAT ARE YOUR LIMITS: THE THINGS YOU DON'T WANT TO BE TRADED. It is about establishing goals and determining limits, both quantitative and qualitative. It is not about going to a negotiation where you not only don't get what you wanted in the beginning but also you grant or accept variables that put you in a much worse position than the one you had when you went to negotiate.

It is often a very common mistake to go to negotiations without any previous work, which makes you go throughout the comings and goings of any negotiation. It is crucial in this regard that before sitting at a table to negotiate we perform an exercise of perspective to be perfectly aware, even before getting there, of what will be the object of negotiation, what we expect to achieve in it and what is our current situation, our starting point. So that, in the event of negotiation movements, we can guarantee that these are given in the right direction, that is moving forward, instead of unconsciously incurring in progressive losses that will result in a worse situation than the one we had before going to negotiate.

So, reflection and previous work, perspective and knowing your objectives and lower limits. Once that is done, it is about moving within that scenario of maximum objectives and limits, which finally most likely will end up in a game space whose limits won't be other than your lower limits, on the one hand, and the limits of your opponent, on the other. Is in this field where you have to know how to move. And it is establishing previously the limits how the game scenario is set up.

Once this is defined the game of concessions exchange would come, with the ultimate aspiration of getting high-value items for me in return for concessions on my part not harmful for me. In such a way that both parties can conclude the negotiation with the satisfaction of the work done, without the sensation of having been manipulated.

3. "LUCK IS WHAT HAPPENS WHEN PREPARATION MEETS OPPORTUNITY" (VOLTAIRE)

People are given to having prejudices. Prejudices that, in case of others success, allow us (we think) to draw conclusions and determine the reasons for third parties good results. When a person is successful the truth is that we don't know the reasons that have led him to that success because generally we only know the result but not the reasons. However, this doesn't prevent us from drawing generally wrong conclusions from the reasons that have caused it.

And this is so because **we tend to apply rational explanations to unknown things**. However, when a person seeks a rational explanation to something, unconsciously does so under his exclusive point of view: what is rational for him in terms of his own experience. But that conclusion is a partial, biased, and arbitrary conclusion. So **what is rational for you doesn't mean it has presumption of truthfulness. It is simply your criterion**.

Therefore, when a person succeeds in something he doesn't do so for what third parties may consider (generally they are reasons of pejorative nature), but because there are reasons and circumstances that people doesn't know but which actually happen, regardless of external valuations.

But, what are those reasons and circumstances? As I have said in the previous paragraph the specific reasons are difficult to know, however, in success cases there is always a common element. A connection point. And in negotiation is not different.

It is a moment when an element outside your control (OPPORTUNITY) coincides with something that is under you control: PREPARATION. What can we conclude with this? One thing is clear: **regardless of the context in which you are, the lack of opportunities that you believe you are having or the few opportunities that have arisen, you always have the faculty and the power to prepare yourself properly for when that opportunity is effectively given**.

From the negotiation point of view you don't know how is going to be. You may have an idea, a certain approximation of how is going to result; but the truth is that the negotiation a priori is uncertain.

But that is not a reason to face the negotiation passively. Quite the opposite. PREPARATION IS THE ONLY THING UNDER YOUR CONTROL. Therefore, the more prepared you are regarding the variables that might arise in the negotiation, the more prepared you are according to your objectives, unquestionable elements and minimum limits, the more possibilities there will be to face the negotiation with more success guarantees in case opportunity appears. In short, success is not a matter of luck. Success, luck in general, and especially in negotiation, is reduced to that moment where an opportunity, beyond your control, coincides with your preparation, which does depend exclusively on you.

TIP 3

"BE PREPARED FOR WHEN OPPORTUNITY APPEARS"

4. <u>"WHERE YOU CAN'T LOVE DON'T DELAY" (FRIDA KAHLO)</u>

Who hasn't been in situations where it is impossible to move forward? Situations where no one gives up. In the end, behaviors like this result in enclosed positions that prevent the negotiation from moving forward, preventing any good result.

As we have said before, negotiating is exchanging. Many consider that when negotiating you must always give up something, but this statement is half-truth. It is true that you have to give up something, but you always have to do so in return for something.

Concessions have an important implicit question: THE MULTIPLICITY OF NEGOTIABLE VARIABLES.

When a negotiation is at an impasse, when it doesn't move forward, when it is stuck, it is usually because negotiators have acquired inflexible positions, but mainly because they are intolerant about a single issue. So that, if you only have an aspiration, it is that thing or nothing, regardless of whether the opponent agrees or not with your aspiration. What is not usually so. Hence the usual blocking. This type of situations usually happen when there is only one negotiation variable, and this is usually money. When it is exclusively a matter of price.

In a negotiation where one party wants to buy as cheaply as possible, and the other wants the opposite, that is, selling it as expensive as possible, with no more possible variables than price, that usually ends up with no agreement or with the situation blocked waiting for the moment where the opponent may falter in his demands for a matter of time and despair.

But what if, apart from price, there were other negotiation variables? What would happen if, starting from the initial positions of buying cheap, on the one hand, and selling expensive, on the other, we introduce, for example, payment times, refund periods, warranty periods, etc.? It wouldn't be the same, would it? So that, if there is no agreement on price you could say "ok, I pay you a little more than I was initially willing to give you, however, in return you have to allow me installment payment." If he pressures you a little more? You can ask for an extension of the warranty period, etc.

As you can see, YOU HAVE TO ENRICH THE NEGOTIATION BY INTRODUCING NEGOTIABLE VARIABLES. Variables that allow the possibility that both parties could be satisfied beyond an exclusive price issue. However, such negotiation variables should always be placed in the game scenario that has been previously settled. **Variables always have to move between the intended objective and the acceptable minimum**. To this end, pre-negotiation preparation is crucial.

TIP 4

"INTRODUCING MULTIPLE NEGOTIABLE VARIABLES IN THE NEGOTIATION"

5. "THERE ARE NO UNINTERESTING THINGS, ONLY UNINTERESTED PEOPLE" (GILBERT KEITH CHESTERTON)

There is one thing that everyone should be aware of in general, and in negotiation in particular: WE HAVE TO SEPARATE INTERESTS FROM POSITIONS. But what is that?

Well, we could say that **positions are what is visible, the request itself**. What is obvious by express desire of the counterpart. However, **interest is what motivates the**

12

position that is adopted. It's the hidden intention, what is implicit in any posture that is adopted.

And I say that we must know how to separate the two elements very well because not doing so can lead to confusion and to adopt the wrong resolutions and attitudes that can ruin the negotiation. All that for not knowing, or not having understood well, what the counterpart is really looking for.

Very often we get carried away by the attitude of our opponent. It is usual that with his attitude, his requests and, in general, with the position that he adopts we take stock of the situation and we could have an uncontrollable tendency to make value judgments. These value judgments make us mistakenly believe we know what the other party is looking for.

However, the positions adopted are still a representation, in a theatrical sense, whose motivation is perfectly hidden and safe. And in negotiation it's this inner motivation that determines everything else, what we are truly interested in knowing. Let us imagine the following situation: two former schoolmates who for different reasons stopped seeing each other. One day one of them goes to a furniture store and realizes that the seller is his old schoolmate. When he is negotiating with him a discount he realizes that his old mate, and now seller, does not agree to make the slightest price reduction, adopting an absolutely intransigent attitude. In this particular situation the seller's position is clear: he doesn't want to make his old partner any kind of discount. However, is that the real interest behind that position? Well, it turns out that in the past when both were classmates the one who is now the buyer was disrespectful with the one who is now a seller. In such a way, that in the seller there is still some resentment with the buyer for behaving in the past in a way that, he understands, was not the most correct.

Thus, this simple story exemplifies very well the difference between the position adopted and the underlying interest of that position. The position adopted is that he doesn't want to apply any discount, however, the underlying interest is not to earn more, but is to annoy his partner because of the feeling he has because of past situations. This being so, if the buyer insisted on the discount and started to explain the reasons why such a discount would be good for both of them, he would get nothing. However, if he were able to discover the underlying interest behind his partner's position, he would probably be able to come to the conclusion that it would be better to invite him to have a coffee to talk and solve the differences because his partner really has no problem in granting a small discount. His problem is other.

The question now is, how can we be able to know the true interests that underlie the positions? The answer is

14

asking questions. A lot of questions. But that is another chapter.

TIP 5

"TRY TO KNOW THE INTERESTS THAT ARE BEHIND THE POSITIONS"

6. "TIME IS THE MOST VALUABLE THING A MAN CAN SPEND" (THEOPHRASTUS)

The concept of 'time' has a twofold aspect: it can work as a 'throwing object', as far as arousing time pressure can be one of the most productive techniques, and as a 'psychological variable', which determines attitude and the other party predisposition when facing the negotiation.

IN A NEGOTIATION THE ONE WHO IS IN A HURRY FINISHES LOSING. It's that simple. Rushing is not good. And even less when the opponent doesn't need to hurry.

In any negotiation process you have to respect the moments. You have to be aware that you have to let your own requests mature in others minds, and give yourself time to assimilate the requests that you've been asked for. Each negotiation implies a thorough investigation to, as already has been mentioned in the previous section, go beyond the positions that have been adopted and thus be able to discover the real interests that are motivating those positions.

A person who is in a hurry to finish something, substantially modifies his priorities. When someone is in a negotiation the priority should be the achievement of his aspirations, being aware that for doing so he will need to make certain concessions that can never exceed the limits established a priori. Concentration should be focused on it. However, when someone pursues the negotiation to conclude as soon as possible, when certain times have been set to carry it out, or when the other party has cleverly pushed you to hurry, the focus changes. Unconsciously the priorities change and you forget the ultimate goal that has motivated the negotiation, to focus on the early conclusion of the meeting.

When one of the parties is pressed to decide or terminate promptly, there is an obvious attention distraction that causes the objectives and maximum concessions to be disregarded, to be willing, instead, to accept anything in order to finish as soon as possible. Great mistake.

Similarly, establishing yourself certain times a priori (I'm not saying establishing times to the counterpart) is an absolute waste of time. Simply because there are issues that you should know that are beyond your control. It is a two part thing, so very little can be done to fit in your desires the other party decision-making process and times.

And apart from being a waste of time is absolutely counterproductive. It is so because time comes first over a good agreement, and this is almost always translated into bad agreements with excessive concessions that go far beyond the predefined limits. Not only the objectives themselves are not achieved, but also it ends up in a process of successive concessions that finishes in a progressive surrender to satisfy the other party and finish as soon as possible.

Knowing the importance of the variable time, crucial I would say, the other party will use for his benefit any hint of haste that they guess at the counterpart. Do not hesitate about that. In fact, it is a powerful trading tool.

TIP 6

"NEVER NEGOTIATE IN A HURRY"

7. <u>"THE WORDS 'NEVER', 'ALWAYS', 'EVERYTHING' OR 'NOTHING' ARE DANGEROUS BECAUSE THEY LEAVE NO OPTIONS" (WALTER RISO)</u>

The extremes are not good. Whites or blacks are out of place. But the truth is that the world is full of gray in its various tones. And it is there where the framework of the negotiation is usually located and, consequently, the meeting points.

RESTRICTIVE POSITIONS ARE THE PERFECT EXAMPLE OF INTRANSIGENCE. And intransigence has only one chance of success: that the other party shows weakness and accepts his surrender. Otherwise there will be no negotiation. Not even a minute. Because negotiating is exchanging. However, as already has been said, such exchange must be contingent upon the conclusions of a preparatory work in relation to the objective or objectives sought with the negotiation, and the concessions oneself has decided to offer without affecting the own interests.

When we say 'never', 'always', 'everything' or 'nothing' we give no choice. We don't establish any negotiation framework because we don't give any space to the counterpart where we could find meeting points. My thing or nothing. Either you give up or there is no agreement. Obviously, the same thing can be applied in the opposite direction.

When we use these types of words that show intransigence we are not looking forward to opening a space for negotiation but we are trying to impose. It is a full-fledged imposition. For all these reasons, let's be perfectly clear about our own goals and limits and be prepared to listen to those on the other side. That will determine the game space in which we are going to move and where hypothetically agreement points could be found.

TIP 7

"DO NOT USE TERMS LIKE 'NEVER', 'ALWAYS', 'EVERYTHING' OR 'NOTHING'"

8. "THERE IS NOTHING AS EASY AND USEFUL AS LISTENING A LOT" (JUAN LUIS VIVES)

We have already talked about the importance of establishing a negotiating framework with the aim of finding meeting points within it. However, **such agreements require a bidirectional communication effort**, so that the other party can know what I want, just as we can know what they want.

That wouldn't be possible if we were not willing to **listen**. To listen absolutely everything people want to tell us. In no case should we assume what their objectives are without having heard them from them. In general, we don't let the rest finish talking because we think we know what the other party wants or is going to tell you. With this we make at least two big mistakes. IN THE FIRST PLACE, prejudices lead us to disconnect from the conversation and to not knowing well, therefore, what the other party wants and the concerns that could have, AND, IN SECOND PLACE, we bother and, in some way, we offend the counterpart because we make them feel unworthy, which may cause him to adopt a defensive attitude from then on and not communicate, therefore, all those questions that otherwise he would have asked us.

When we listen and let the other party talk freely we make the other party feel more comfortable and, at the same time, we get an immense amount of information about what he wants and what he is not willing to give up, information on the issues he gives more or less importance, and, more importantly, when talking we can guess concerns or buried desires that can facilitate the knowledge of those real interests that determine his position and, therefore, his requests.

Consequently, we can conclude that **letting the other party talk is key**. Let him talk and listen carefully. That active listening of what they have to tell us is one of the greatest assets we have as negotiators. You have to listen and listen a lot. It is there where we can get relevant information. What's more, WE HAVE TO LISTEN UNTIL THE LAST THING THEY HAVE TO TELL US. Because it is precisely at the end, when fatigue begins, when the most relevant is usually said: those things of greater content and substance. In short, we should let people talk, and listen very carefully to what they have to say.

TIP 8

"LISTEN TO EVERYTHING PEOPLE HAVE TO TELL US"

9. "BEING QUIET IS MORE THAN NOT TALKING" (ROBERT FISHER)

KNOWING HOW TO REMAIN QUIET IS ONE OF THE GREATEST VIRTUES A PERSON CAN HAVE. As people we tend to fill the silences of conversations with some kind of comment because we understand that those periods of silence are deeply uncomfortable. And it is true that they often are.

However, when a person is able to remain quiet for a period of time he communicates more things than if, on the contrary, he was talking. The silences express a multitude of things and are an obvious sign of respect for the necessary periods of reflection that the other party may need.

On many occasions, when we make certain assertions we are not able to wait for the other's response if we understand that the response is taking too long. And we don't, FIRST, because we feel uncomfortable waiting. SECOND, because we can't manage the anxiety and uncertainty of the lack of response. AND THIRD, because we want to justify, unduly and unnecessarily, our arguments in order to condition the counterpart response. Such behavior, regardless of not respecting the times of the one who needs to think about what he has heard, also indicates something else. Let's call it anxiety, distress, or worry.

In fact, an experienced negotiator will do just that. Keep silent about any issue that may arise. At least in the beginning. And it will do so for the purpose of calibrating the opponent. To know to what extent it is a strong positioning or not. Because silence at certain times is understood as something equivalent to firmness, but not intransigence.

When a negotiator poses a certain position and is unable to stay quiet afterwards waiting for a reply, providing unnecessary justifications and explanations in between, it denotes psychological fragility and weakness in argumentation. Because of all this, silence, or in this case his lack, gives a lot of information to the other party that can use later in his favor. Conversely, the ability to remain silent denotes firmness and determination, and an absolute emotional control over the situation.

TIP 9

"SILENCE, OR THE LACK OF IT, PROVIDES MANY TIMES MORE INFORMATION THAN A WORD"

10. "THE YIELDING OF THE WEAK IS THE CONCESSION TO FEAR" (EDMUND BURKE)

Another question is being able to know the concession reasons. If it's really about concessions that you had previously considered, or if, on the contrary, it is about concessions motivated by fear.

A very frequent mistake is disconnecting from the real reasons to which a given concession has to respond. Let's not forget that the objective is to achieve a goal and that in order to get so it will be necessary to make concessions that previously have been studied and accepted as possible. CONCESSIONS NEED TO HAVE A UTILITARIAN PURPOSE WITHIN THE NEGOTIATION.

However, concessions often respond to purely psychological questions, to an unconscious feeling of insecurity that generally translates into an inferiority complex. This pushes us to want to please the counterpart forgetting our own interests and what we are really looking for with the negotiation.

Not only concessions do not respond to what they really should respond to, but they also have a not consensual impulsive character. This is what causes very bad concessions for our interests and absolutely hasty.

When concessions are the reflection of wanting to please the other party they are usually characterized by two elements. IN THE FIRST PLACE, by its **arbitrariness**, that is, the concession responds to specific caprices and not to rational principles stipulated a priori in the preparation of the negotiation. AND, IN SECOND PLACE, because that spirit of wanting to please causes that, **each time, the magnitude of the concession made is very important**.

When it comes to making concessions, it shouldn't be forgotten that they should be duly considered in advance, and that their size, the size of the concession, should be small each time. **Small concessions must always be made instead of large ones**. And the latter are those that are made when they are backed by purely emotional criteria. And we shouldn't forget that in the end our goal as negotiators should be achieving great goals each time in return for small concessions.

TIP 10

"FEAR INVITES TO MAKE EXCESSIVE CONCESSIONS"

11. "INNOVATION IS NOT ABOUT SAYING YES TO EVERYTHING. IT'S ABOUT SAYING NO TO ALL BUT THE MOST CRUCIAL FEATURES" (STEVE JOBS)

One of the most appreciated characteristics of those who are considered as expert negotiators is the ability to say 'no'.

Saying 'no' is the beginning of the negotiation. In the initial statements that the other party makes, the most common thing is to say 'no'. It is natural not to accept in the beginning the initial requests of the other party because we would enter into a mere acceptance of others requirements. **Saying 'no' prevents others, positions yourself as interlocutor and invites the other party to have a particular consideration about you.** THAT FIRST 'NO' IS A STRENGTH METER, is a way of saying, without saying it, that things aren't going to be easy. In fact, the reputation of hard negotiators that some have is concretely due to the frequency with which they use this word. The word 'No'.

We have already said that saying 'no' positions yourself, creates you a brand image, but is not limited to that. Saying 'no' invites the other party to consider your pretensions equally. It forces to dig further into your requests and to seek meeting points.

Many new negotiators are afraid of using the word 'no'. And it is not exclusively a negotiation issue. Moreover, it is a people psychological variable that transcends and affects negotiations. At the moment of saying 'no' there is an implicit fear. A fear that has its answer in the aversion to rejection, in the pathological desire of the human being to please others. We all personally take very seriously the possibility of not liking others, of disappointing, of not fulfilling expectations. Therefore, our natural tendency is to satisfy others but, not for their own satisfaction, but because their satisfaction implicitly brings our emotional well-being. In life and in negotiation this is the main reason why it is so difficult for us to say 'no'. Which is a weakness of relative importance and that any skilled negotiator is able to see quickly and, consequently, take advantage of it.

However, for those who, even knowing their natural limitation of not knowing, or not being able to say 'no', there are tools or methods that allow them to save that blocking. One of them is that, given the impossibility of accepting certain conditions posed by the other party, and the discomfort that would imply to say 'no' from an emotional point of view, giving answers to those requests that are obviously unrealizable or inconceivable for those who listen those answers. Let them, and not you, come to the conclusion. Or they do so, or they would do things that would suppose shooting themselves in the foot.

TIP 11

12. "IT ALWAYS HURTS MORE TO HAVE AND LOSE THAN TO NOT HAVE IN THE FIRST PLACE" (KHALED HOSSEINI)

Negotiating has a lot to do with the psychological game. Independently of previous preparation, it is frequent to create yourself expectations related to the negotiation. It is obvious that you are negotiating for a specific reason, and it is also common to visualize what would be a good result for your interests.

Expert negotiators know that and know as well how to exploit it. They know how to feed the expectations of new negotiators and encourage them to visualize a reality that isn't yet, but that makes them think it's almost there.

And it is when you are already in that situation when demands begin. All the 'yes but ...', 'ok but now ...', 'it is true that it is almost done but ...' begin to appear. In short, they cause psychological variables play against you in order to create you a greater 'PAIN'.

It's not the same facing a negotiation without expectation, that is, only focusing on what we must do to achieve our interests, than being with the goals already gained and feel the threat of losing them. **From an emotional point of view, it is not the same not having something but knowing the possibility of having it, than already having it and knowing the possibility of losing it.** It's much more painful to lose something that is already yours, or you understand that already is, than never having it.

Good negotiators are able to discover what causes pain in the opponent to squeeze it according to their interests. THEY SEARCH THE 'PAIN' AND SQUEEZE. And they do so because instinctively, once there is pain, the human being tends to get rid of it as quickly as possible. And speed has a lot to do with the lack of patience, with the lack of judgment and the lack of analysis. What results in mistaken, hasty decisions; and consequently benefits our opponent.

TIP 12

"IT HURTS MORE LOSING WHAT YOU ALREADY HAVE RATHER THAN NOT GETTING WHAT YOU WANT"

13. "CHEOPS' LAW: NOTHING EVER GETS BUILT ON SCHEDULE OR WITHIN BUDGET" (ROBERT HEINLEIN)

As in any other thing, you need to have a look to the budget. Yes, also when dealing with a negotiation all the costs in which you may incur must be budgeted, and know to what extent you can negotiate from the budgetary point of view.

Jim Camp explains it very well. Negotiations have important expenses, not only economic, but also other. Specifically, the costs to be considered in advance, and which should also be limited, are: THE ECONOMIC COST, THE TIME COST and THE EMOTIONAL COST.

At the beginning the most common thing is thinking that it is the economic cost that acquires greater relevance because of its monetary character, but nothing further from reality. Indeed it can be so but we would do well not ignoring the other two costs.

The importance of each of them will result from the resources that can be allocated to each of these matters. In such a way that there will be situations where if the period of negotiation is going to get too long that won't mean a significant economic offense given the solvency we may have. However, the cost of time can be a problem because at some point it may be what we lack. And so we could say about the emotional cost: we have money, we have time too, however, it is the psychological thing what can affect most when carrying a negotiation to a good end.

Therefore, **we must always consider the three variables together**. It's not about analyzing them separately. It's an addition. Everything has to be considered in the balance. LET'S SET WHAT BUDGET WE CAN ASSUME TRYING TO BE SMALLER THAN OUR OPPONENTS. We could use as well the knowledge of the variables that make up the budget to voluntarily increase the opponents budget item that we consider may be more beneficial for our interests. An example of this would be to make the counterpart be the one who travels permanently to the negotiation while we negotiate in our facilities. In this situation, who do you think could be more ready to delay negotiations, the part that has to move permanently and book hotels, or the one that doesn't have to do so?

TIP 13

"MINIMIZE YOUR COSTS AND INCREASE THE COSTS OF YOUR OPPONENT"

PART II: THE INNER GAME (PSYCHOLOGY)

14. "MASTERING OTHERS IS STRENGTH. MASTERING YOURSELF IS TRUE POWER" (LAO TSE)

The sentence that gives name to this part exemplifies what could be considered as one of the most important faculties, if not the most, that any negotiator should have. This faculty is the capacity of SELF-CONTROL.

Self-control is key, basic, crucial. Put the adjective that you consider best. Self-control is the common denominator of the other capacities that are developed here in the different sections. Without self-control everything else disappears, it won't exist or it won't be performed properly.

SEL-CONTROL IS AN EMOTIONAL SELF-MANAGEMENT QUALITY. Being able to self-control doesn't mean avoiding the emotions; it is not about ignoring your worries or your philias and phobias. No. It is rather **an exercise of self-awareness and self-reflection**. It's being able to be aware of what happens to you and how you feel so that in that state of consciousness we can manage it in the most appropriate way possible according to our interests. Self-control means not losing your nerves when facing aggressions from others, regardless of whether your feelings invite you to do the opposite. It's being able to put a stop to those emotional issues that may be counterproductive. But it's not easy. And it is not because,

31

to a certain extent, it is about acting against nature. On the contrary to what your instincts want. It is therefore much easier to explain this capacity as what it should be done but, nevertheless, is extremely difficult to put into practice. In such a way that there are not many who acquire this quality in moments of enormous tension and for that reason we especially admire people who have those faculties.

IT'S THIS HUGE COMPLEXITY THAT MEANS ACQUIRING THIS CAPACITY WHICH MAKES IT THE PERFECT TOOL FOR EXPERT NEGOTIATORS. Usually they use it to make the counterpart lose good temper, so that they lose with the forms the reason they might have in the background; and to move away as far as possible the reason from the opponents criterion.

When you lose self-control you lose everything else. The visceral prevails over the rational. And that means losing credibility and making bad decisions, usually in a very hasty way.

TIP 14

"SELF-CONTROL"

15. "REASON WITHOUT UNDERSTANDING IS LIKE CUPID WITHOUT HEART" (JUAN LOBILLO)

WHAT YOU THINK REALLY DOESN'T MATTER. It's that simple. Such statement may sound surprising, but nothing further from reality. **What really matters is what the other party thinks**. What is relevant is the perception the other party has about the facts.

A very common mistake when dealing with a negotiation is adopting a reductionist thinking about it. To limit yourself to your own concerns, positions, opinions and requests without considering the other side situation. We tend to think that our opinions and positions according to a given context must be shared. We prejudge thoughts and behaviors with the argument that in similar situations everyone should behave the same way. We presume it without consulting and, consequently, we fall into a great error.

It is difficult for us to practice what we preach by example. Empathy is a good example of this. It is one of those words absolutely worn out by its verbal use but which, however, has a very limited application from a practical point of view. In reality we use to perfectly conjugate the 'me, mine, with me', and we don't have problems to evaluate other people's behaviors in a pejorative way if the positions, opinions and behaviors of others are not as ours in the same situation. But how can you think that! If it is very clear that it is like that!

Such an expression denotes an absolute lack of empathy. A lack of interest in really knowing what others behavior is. The main principle is the following: if you don't know something, ask. If you don't understand certain behaviors, ask. If you can't find explanation for certain questions, ask. In short: ASK.

And you must ask because, as we said at the beginning of the section, your opinion doesn't matter. The opinion that really matters is the one of the other side of the negotiation! If not, how do you pretend to reach an agreement without understanding the other party? This way the agreement will never come. For the agreement to come, the counterpart must be convinced that it is the best deal. It is his opinion, and not yours, that determines whether it is or not. It is his perception that will give, or not, free way to the agreement. It won't be your request in any case.

So, the next time you're going to consider that something 'doesn't make sense', perhaps you should stop and think that the fact that 'doesn't make sense' to you doesn't mean that it doesn't to everyone else. Try to find out what sense can be. You'll be closer to reaching an agreement.

TIP 15

"IF SOMETHING DOESN'T MAKE SENSE FOR YOU DOESN'T MEAN THAT IT DOESN'T MAKE SENSE FOR OTHER"

16. <u>"FEAR RULES LIFE" (ALBERT SCHWEITZER)</u>

PEOPLE CAN LISTEN WHAT YOU SAY BUT ONLY REACT TO FEAR. It is a fact. Negotiating has a lot to do with being a doctor. Not because the activity itself but yes by analogy. **In negotiation, as in medicine, you must look for where it hurts and then tighten**.

People only react to two things: the possibility of profit and the possibility of loss, being the latter the most powerful of the two. People react more to the possibility of loss than to the possibility of profit. Let's say that, generally, losing gives much more fear.

But fear doesn't need to appear for a reason. It is more a mental projection. It is more a painful anticipation of a future hypothesis. As species, we are certainty fervent admirers and, therefore, we are suspicious about anything that may question it.

In this way, EXPERT NEGOTIATORS ANALYSE THE OPPONENT WITH THE OBJECTIVE OF FINDING HIS PARTICULAR 'PAIN' TO SQUEEZE IT TO THE MAXIMUM. In the pursuit of convincing the opponent we won't achieve anything if our argument doesn't focus especially on his 'pain', on what concerns him, on what he is afraid of. Let's not forget that, as I said at the beginning, **people do not react to words, they do react to pain**, and pain has a close relationship with concerns, fears and needs.

TIP 16

"DISCOVER YOUR OPPONENTS' 'PAIN'"

17. "FOR BIG THINGS A LONG TIME IS REQUIRED" (SÉNECA)

We have already talked about it. As expert negotiators it is important to understand the significance of the knowledge of the use of the TIME variable not only as a technique but also in its psychological variable. You already know that **the lack of time in the negotiation causes everything to hurry, so it would be good to give us time to negotiate**.

On the contrary, it is interesting to arouse certain urgency in the opposite party to make him feel in a hurry. When there is time availability, or when it is projected the possibility of having it, it favors two issues. IN THE FIRST PLACE, it is transmitted such a resistance that can arouse some respect or fear in the opponent because the possibility of facing a long negotiation, with all the fatigue that entails. And this, before starting, causes in the opposite party some laziness and previous weariness.

And IN THE SECOND PLACE, when we show time disposition, and that we have no urgency to negotiate, we place in the ideology of the opposing party the idea that we are calm, serene, careful and responsible. All of them qualities that along with the first of the points said already create certain hopelessness in the opponent. The game hasn't started yet and we are already winning.

However, these characteristics have to be sustainable throughout the negotiation in order to confirm the worst omens of the counterpart and to be able to progressively diminish their spirit. Projecting this quality is not an easy thing if we take into consideration the back and forth that will undoubtedly arise throughout the negotiation.

If we are the ones who have to face someone who has, or says he has, an infinite patience, either we need to have the same faculty and we let it know to the opposite party, or it would be better to wait and negotiate when better chances may appear if it is true that time is what we are not going to have. **Do not let people urge you to negotiate quickly. Do not accept time constraints from the opposing party. Neither deadlines**. Everything must be done without haste, with time, regardless the other negotiating party likes it or not.

TIP 17

"THE CONTRARY PART WILL SEE HIS MORAL UNDERMINED IF PERCEIVES YOUR TIME AVAILABILITY"

18. "IF YOUR PROBLEM HAS A SOLUTION THEN… WHY WORRY ABOUT IT? IF YOUR PROBLEM DOESN'T HAVE SOLUTION THEN… WHY WORRY ABOUT IT?" (CHINESE PROVERB)

ONE OF THE THINGS THAT STRESSES MOST IS ANTICIPATING THE RESULT. Rather, anticipate the result consequences. And I will go further: to anticipate the consequences of a bad result, or, directly, the lack of any result.

It's as if from a mental point of view we gave a jump directly to the future avoiding the negotiation itself and all that it involves. This is absolutely normal. After all, any negotiation has a specific purpose, and that is achieving what you want or not. Something that will qualify the performance of those who have taken part. The negotiation strategy is always submitted to the achievement of a series of objectives. Otherwise, negotiating would make no sense.

However, success in negotiation capitulates to this PARADOX: **the purpose of the negotiation should not determine our attention, but yes our own performance in the negotiation process**. WHY? **The result doesn't depend only on us. What does depend on us is to execute all those matters that are in our hands, and that depend exclusively on us, to try to carry out the negotiation successfully**. CONCERNING ABOUT THE RESULT IS

USELESS, given that it depends as well on the counterparty's decision. That being said, preparing yourself, investigating, staying informed, asking, listening, adopting a calm and empathetic posture ... those are elements, all of them, that depend exclusively on oneself. And it's precisely there where we must focus on. Our concentration must be focused on those things that are in our hands. The result absolutely escapes to us.

And that is why it stresses us so much. It's a tremendously uncertain element, but which at the same time is the central element of the negotiation and the reason why it has been carried out.

Therefore, the title of this section. From a practical point of view it is useless to worry about things that are beyond our control, but yes it is useful to worry about those things that are under our control.

TIP 18

"FOCUS EXCLUSIVELY ON WHAT IS UNDER YOUR CONTROL"

19. "NOBODY OFFERS AS MUCH AS THE ONE WHO WILL NOT FULFILL" (FRANCISCO DE QUEVEDO)

When negotiating, promises are the art of interested procrastination. The one who promises enters into the game of psychological persuasion. I can't give it now, but I promise to give it in the future. Usually it works quite well. It is a powerful persuasion tool because affects the innate belief of others benevolence. We believe because instinctively we want to believe.

To distrust others is a learned feeling, whose teacher is the experience in all its cruelty. When we negotiate with someone who shows a conciliatory attitude, unconsciously, we believe we are in a collaboration scenario where good faith is presupposed. Nothing is further from reality.

Expert negotiators work conscientiously on the counterpart predisposition. They establish a supposedly collaborative framework to 'feed' mutual trust. They manipulate in a Machiavellian way so that the counterpart creates himself an illusory reality.

It's that perfectly worked collaborative framework which gives credibility to the promise. An interested promise. Where what is pursued is a present commitment in exchange for a future promise. And guess what: the future promise is never given. However the commitment is already acquired.

CONCESSIONS AND COMMITMENTS ALWAYS HAVE TO BE GIVEN IN THE SAME TEMPORARY SPACE. ALWAYS. If not, we will be permanently opened to deception.

TIP 19

"DO NOT CONCEDE AND DO NOT COMMIT YOURSELF IN RETURN FOR FUTURE PROMISES"

20. "THE ONLY GOOD PARTS OF A BOOK ARE THE EXPLANATIONS THAT HAVE BEEN OMITTED IN IT" (BAUDELAIRE)

It is very common that when putting our requests on the table we tend to not expose them directly. We are just accustomed to 'dress' them with justifications that support those requests. We don't feel comfortable transmitting what we want. Doing so would entail a feeling of personal discomfort.

So, we would do well if we get rid of that feeling. **Behind the excessive justifications and explanations rests a feeling of guilt**. We understand that any approach we make should be subjected to reasons according to the opponent. However, the counterpart is not about that he doesn't listen to reasons, but that he listens exclusively to his own reasons.

When we exceed ourselves with justifications and explanations, we do so because we understand that it is the right way to proceed. In order to show that our pretensions are not crazy and have their explanation. However, WHAT REALLY UNDERLIES IN THE EXCESS OF EXPLANATIONS AND JUSTIFICATIONS IS A LACK OF SELF-CONFIDENCE. An insecurity that the opponent will surely know how to interpret according to his interests.

Therefore, giving too many explanations about what we demand shows, FIRSTLY, a certain psychological weakness, and, IN SECOND PLACE, favors the transmission of 'free' and not necessary information that could be used subsequently against us.

In short, in an exercise of assertiveness and strength, let's limit ourselves to putting forward what we expect with a succinct explanation. No justifications in any case. They are neither practical nor good unlike what we might believe.

TIP 20

"DO NOT JUSTIFY YOURSELF"

21. "TEMPERANCE IS THE VIGOR OF SOUL" (JAIME BALMES)

We are perhaps in front of one of the most important faculties when it comes to negotiating. TEMPERANCE AS SOMETHING ABSOLUTELY ESSENTIAL. However, its degree of importance is directly proportional to the scarcity of its application.

It is evident that **temperance and self-control go hand in hand**. The first one implies the second one, with self-control being a broader concept than temperance. The lack of temperance translates into hostile behaviors towards the opponent including aggressive and somewhat quarrelsome voice tones. What is really desirable in any negotiation is KEEPING AN ATTITUDE AS NEUTRAL AS

POSSIBLE. Both behavior and tone. We must stick exclusively to what we have come to. The rest is only a misdirection that distances us from the right path preset that can be totally counterproductive.

It is about adopting an attitude and a tone with the necessary perspective. Of healthy objectivity. Let both conduct and voice be calm, without raising the voice, and with the most neutral rictus possible.

TEMPERANCE, in short, behaves as a CORRECTING EFFECT of those primary impulses that could happen at any moment. It is the faculty of 'auto-filing' the emotional asperities that each one of us could have to limit to the fundamental.

For all this, let us adopt our most neutral and undaunted attitude possible. A behavior according to what we are concerned with. That turns around the object of the negotiation. The rest it is only noise.

TIP 21

"ADOPT A CALM ATTITUDE"

22. "DO NOT MIX APPLES WITH ORANGES" (PROVERB)

Very much in relation to the previous section, it is very common in negotiations to lose your temper when facing incomprehensible approaches and attitudes from the opposite party.

Any negotiation altercation invite, from the most visceral, to take things personally. What are discussions that affect the subject that is being negotiated end up being conceived as personal attacks, in a way that you end up having a distorted view of reality. In a scenario where reason must prevail, it ends up turning around the reciprocal unrest.

When this purely emotional attitude is adopted you move away from the objective precepts that have led to the negotiation and that are sought with it, to try to respond to our emotional situation towards the opponent. Something that clearly has nothing to do with the purpose of the negotiation.

TAKING THINGS PERSONALLY ENPHASIZES OUR VULNERABILITY. It is giving our opponent a lot of scope so that we will surrender to his plans. All this because the control loss. The control of what is being the object of discussion, and your own control that makes you not listen to reasons; that makes you fall into thoughtlessness, irrationality and the lack of sanity.

Such behavior changes the focus of what is important. It transfers the importance to the most irrelevant from what is actually the most important: the negotiation object. We focus on the 'messenger' instead of the 'message'. We lose the criterion to go back to Paleolithic stages where the head had little to do and yes, instead, the instinctive.

The reality of a negotiation is that two parties meet around an object of discussion with the goal of reaching satisfactory agreements, shared and assumed by both parties.

TIP 22

"DO NOT TAKE THINGS PERSONALLY. LEAVE PERSONAL THINGS ASIDE"

23. "THINGS ARE ONLY WORTH WHAT YOU MAKE THEM WORTH" (MOLIÈRE)

MAKE PEOPLE RESPECT YOU. DO NOT TRY TO BE LIKED. This, that looks like a truism is one of the most difficult things to accomplish. It is so because we are talking about something purely instinctive.

There is a human being natural predisposition to seek others acceptance. We tend to seek harmony in our relationships and it is terribly painful for us if that harmony is truncated. As a consequence we are instinctively more

46

pleasant and condescending to others position, while unconsciously we ignore our principles, goals and limits. Everything with the ultimate goal of being liked by the opposite party.

Such behaviors lead us, figuratively, to disregard the role that, as negotiators, is expected from us. Are the expert negotiators who immediately perceive this need to please the other party and, thus, take advantage of it.

You don't go to a negotiation to make friends or please anyone. You go for what you go. It is about finding a solution for a specific issue with whom both parties are ok. For that it is crucial to make people respect you. Even far above other considerations. They should see us as equals. Moreover, I would say that it is much more beneficial to make them be afraid of you rather than make them see you as someone friendly. A fear that comes from respect and the purest assertiveness.

Obviously is much easier saying it than doing it, like all those things that are merely instinctive. Now, not being easy doesn't mean that we reject what we may be interested in because considering it 'too difficult'. The mere fact of knowing this natural tendency to seek the others acceptance has to serve as a warning so that, when this happens, we can put all the tools within our reach to change the behavior and consciously take up the position most appropriate to our interests.

"MAKE PEOPLE RESPECT YOU"

24. "DISCRETION IS THE BETTER PART OF VALOR" (WILLIAM SHAKESPEARE)

Discretion is not only a matter exclusively applicable to negotiation. We are talking about something that should prevail in all the things in life.

When we talk about discretion we talk about prudence, about caution, about good sense. About adopting a low profile regardless of what your life presents you. As humans we are very much given to extremes. We tend to give a special relevance to everything that happens in our life that gets out of the everyday and usual.

Many people like to 'dress' joys and sorrows with admiration signs, when you are wealthy and when you are not, and, especially, we are given to make special ostentation of knowledge under the wrong belief that it will favor our acceptance and the valuation that others will make of our person.

It's this last point that becomes especially relevant in negotiations. And it is because of the uncontrollable desire of our ego to be constantly fed that we usually surrender to one of our main instincts: THE FEELING OF IMPORTANCE.

We mistakenly believe that in order for our aspiration to be admirable according to others, we must demonstrate it at every moment. As a consequence we tend to provide information and demonstrate knowledge that either it is not the subject of the negotiation or is information that the other party doesn't need to know. And even if it is not necessary for the other party to know it, he does it, that can only indicate one thing: that there is a risk of giving the other party information that could be used against us. Likewise, making ostentation of your faculties, of your possessions or other things only causes one thing: generating prejudices in the other party that can dynamite the negotiation.

Personally I apply a principle whenever I have doubts about whether saying or not saying certain information: ¿SAYING SUCH INFORMATION CAN BE BENEFICIAL FOR ME? If the answer is 'NO' I ask myself the following: IF I SAY IT, THAT MAY AFFECT ME NEGATIVELY IN THE FUTURE? And if the answer is 'yes' I don't say it and I stay quiet.

TIP 24

"BE ALWAYS DISCREET"

25. "NECESSITY NEVER MADE GOOD BARGAIN" (BENJAMIN FRANKLIN)

I don't discover anything new if I say that when someone deals with a negotiation it does it with a certain objective, even knowing that in order to obtain it he has to yield in some questions so that the counterpart can obtain something of his interest.

This being so, it is also true that, as we have discussed before, the negotiation is an exchange process. It is true that it must be bidirectional. If it is not, we would not be talking about an exchange itself but a unilateral surrender.

Obviously nobody likes to surrender. However, whether or not this is so will depend on the degree of need that the other party feels that you have to reach an agreement. **The more need you show, the more demands and concessions the other party will ask for**. It is also true that it is possible that this need really exists and that you are willing to get what you long for. Now, DON'T SHOW THAT NEED. If necessary, act. And do it so that it seems that **you would like to reach that agreement but that in no case you need it**. So that if the negotiation doesn't run along the paths that you understand adequate there is no problem in getting up from the table and leave.

If, on the contrary, they see your need they will know where your particular 'pain' is. And they will squeeze you. They will press where it hurts you most in the form of requests and demands. All that with the aim of, in exchange for getting rid of what oppresses and hurts you, getting everything he asked you for.

As a consequence we may find ourselves in a scenario where a person goes to a negotiation under certain conditions, with the need to reach a concrete agreement, and concludes it by obtaining only what he intended but in exchange for a multitude of issues that he already possessed and that he didn't contemplate losing. In such a way that he has lost much more than he has won. He has ended up selling the car to buy gas.

TIP 25

"INTEREST IN COMING TO AN AGREEMENT: YES. NEED TO COME TO IT: IN NO EVENT"

26. "TO WHOM CAN'T SAVE HIMSELF NOBODY CAN SAVE" (CESARE PAVESE)

Sometimes empathy exercises can be counterproductive. It has always been said that empathy is a virtue, but it is so only if your own limits are respected, your interests.

Generally there is a diffuse border between what is empathy, understood as the faculty of putting oneself in the place of the other, and the innate will to be liked by others. Because deep down, as human beings, we take it

51

hard to see the possibility to be disliked by somebody. That's why the unconscious and quasi-pathological quest to seek others acceptance.

WHY DO WE CALL IT EMPATHY WHEN WE WANT TO SAY OTHERS ACCEPTANCE? In any negotiation there may be circumstances in which, according to the approaches made, it is evident that the counterparty is in trouble. In this situation many people feel uncomfortable and decide to make concessions or soften the approaches made with the ultimate goal of getting the other party out of the predicament in which he is. Somehow they 'save his face' under the wrong autosuggesting argument that it is really an exercise of empathy worthy of praise.

But what is certain is that this is a mistake. **We must never 'save the face' to others**. You go to a negotiation being aware of the objective you have and having perfectly clear the limits and the possible concessions. It is evident that what is posed to arrive to this objective can generate tensions in the other part. However, IT IS NONE OF OUR BUSINESS TO FACILITATE OTHER PEOPLE'S DECISIONS FOR INCOMODITY REASONS. It is the other party that, if necessary, will have to decide what he can or can't do in this respect and that's why we will have to give the other party a reasonable time so he can take the decision he thinks is better for this new reality.

Let's not forget that **taking the other party from the predicament you have created for him will be perceived by the counterpart as an emotional weakness, and he could therefore make an interested use of it to achieve what he wants in the future**.

TIP 26

"DO NOT 'SAVE THE FACE' TO THE CONTRARY PART"

27. "GOD TEMPERS THE WIND TO THE SHORN LAMB" (PROVERB)

It is obvious saying that throughout a negotiation there are lots of ups and downs. Many moves that usually find their replies in the counterpart. However, there are times when a negotiator is aware that he has the other party between a rock and a hard place. Moments where there is no possible reply because the other negotiating party lacks a concrete argument against certain approaches.

As negotiators we might think that this situation greatly facilitates the achievement of the negotiating objective. However, although this belief is largely based on the general ideology, far from helping complicates things enormously.

Let's not forget that for a negotiation to succeed it must run in the field of the object that occupies us. However, **if as negotiators we push the other party and we don't stop in the pursuit of leaving the other party without a**

possible exit we can actually get the opposite. We will have hurt his pride. The negotiation will be dynamited and what has been achieved so far will fall on deaf ears. By then the negotiation will have entered into the personal field for the other party consideration and he very possibly will not listen to reasons.

When a person stands between a rock and a hard place, and is unable to see an honorable exit, he displays his most primal, most animal instincts and rises up to get out of that situation, even attacking if he considers so. A person in this situation behaves in the same way as a freshly caught fish: it flaps and attacks because it has nothing to lose anymore.

Therefore, as negotiators do not pester until exhaustion. Do not hurt the counterpart pride. Let the opposing side 'save his face' and have a way out. And I say that he can save his face, not that we have to save it ourselves.

TIP 27

"LEAVE THE OPPONENT ALWAYS A WAY OUT"

28. "IGNORANCE IS LESS REMOTE FROM THE TRUTH THAN PREJUDICE" (DENIS DIDEROT)

This epigraph sentence means a fundamental thing: DO NOT PRESUPPOSE OR PREJUDGE. It's that simple. **As people we feel more comfortable making value judgments of what we see, observe and hear**. Value judgments under the attribute of absolute truths, when the truth is that these judgments, and consequently the presumptions, are always conditioned by the education and experiences that each one of us could have had. Far from axiomatic truths, particular considerations can never be regarded as true truths.

In the sphere of negotiation, presumptions acquire a fundamental importance, insofar as they have perverse effects because they distort reality. WHEN WE PRESUPPOSE THINGS STOP BEING WHAT THEY REALLY ARE TO BE WHAT WE CONSIDER THEY ARE. And that in a negotiation is an incorrect starting point.

Incorrect because we get the stage mixed up. Incorrect because we don't know the true pretensions of the opposing party, as well as his needs, situation and knowledge. **Presumptions make us ignorant under a veil of knowledge**. But presupposing is easy. PRESUPPOSING IS THE RESULT OF EGO PLUS LAZINESS.

To carry out a negotiation, you must be as sure as possible about everything that is part of it. From the scenario where we are negotiating to the real pretensions of the counterpart, considering as well their concerns, needs and his reality. And for this there is only one tool: ASKING. When you are not sure about what he is looking for, ask, do not presuppose. When you don't know what his true needs are, ask, don't presuppose. When you don't know what his reality is, ask, don't presuppose. And so on every time you don't have clear a thing. **Presupposing is easy but it is absolutely inefficient**.

TIP 28

"DO NOT PRESUPPOSE"

PART IV: SUMMARY

1. "NEGOTIATION IS EXCHANGING. IF I GIVE SOMETHING THE COUNTERPARTY MUST GIVE ME SOMETHING, AND IF I ASK FOR SOMETHING, I MUST BE READY TO GIVE SOMETHING"

2. "KNOW BEFORE NEGOTIATING WHAT ARE YOUR OBJECTIVES AND WHAT ARE YOUR LIMITS"

3. "BE PREPARED FOR WHEN OPPORTUNITY APPEARS"

4. "INTRODUCING MULTIPLE NEGOTIABLE VARIABLES IN THE NEGOTIATION"

5. "TRY TO KNOW THE INTERESTS THAT ARE BEHIND THE POSITIONS"

6. "NEVER NEGOTIATE IN A HURRY"

7. "DO NOT USE TERMS LIKE 'NEVER', 'ALWAYS', 'EVERYTHING' OR 'NOTHING'"

8. "LISTEN TO EVERYTHING PEOPLE HAVE TO TELL US"

9. "SILENCE, OR THE LACK OF IT, PROVIDES MANY TIMES MORE INFORMATION THAN A WORD"

10. "FEAR INVITES TO MAKE EXCESSIVE CONCESSIONS"

11. "DARE TO SAY 'NO'"

12. "IT HURTS MORE LOSING WHAT YOU ALREADY HAVE RATHER THAN NOT GETTING WHAT YOU WANT"

13. "MINIMIZE YOUR COSTS AND INCREASE THE COSTS OF YOUR OPPONENT"

14. "SELF-CONTROL"

15. "IF SOMETHING DOESN'T MAKE SENSE FOR YOU DOESN'T MEAN THAT IT DOESN'T MAKE SENSE FOR OTHER"

16. "DISCOVER YOUR OPPONENTS' 'PAIN'"

17. "THE CONTRARY PART WILL SEE HIS MORAL UNDERMINED IF PERCEIVES YOUR TIME AVAILABILITY"

18. "FOCUS EXCLUSIVELY ON WHAT IS UNDER YOUR CONTROL"

19. "DO NOT CONCEDE AND DO NOT COMMIT YOURSELF IN RETURN FOR FUTURE PROMISES"

20. "DO NOT JUSTIFY YOURSELF"

21. "ADOPT A CALM ATTITUDE"

22. "DO NOT TAKE THINGS PERSONALLY. LEAVE PERSONAL THINGS ASIDE"

23. "MAKE PEOPLE RESPECT YOU"

24. "BE ALWAYS DISCREET"

25. "INTEREST IN COMING TO AN AGREEMENT: YES. NEED TO COME TO IT: IN NO EVENT"

26. "DO NOT 'SAVE THE FACE' TO THE CONTRARY PART"

27. "LEAVE THE OPPONENT ALWAYS A WAY OUT"

28. "DO NOT PRESUPPOSE"

Twitter: @PaulFraga

www.futbolydineroresponsable.com